King's Road: for
King and Country

Compiled by
Judy Sutton & Helen Little

Published and available from
TheEndlessBookcase.com

This booklet is available in both paper and electronic format.
Available in multiple e-book formats.

The Endless Bookcase Ltd
Suite 14 Stanta Business Centre, 3 Soothouse Spring
St Albans, Hertfordshire, AL3 6PF, England

ISBN: 978-1-914151-13-2

Reviews

This book is a poignant tribute to a past community by their successors; a vibrant testimony to the strength of both. Memorialisation has been important throughout history in the wake of significant events. This was pre-eminently so in the aftermath of the First World War as communities sought to perpetuate story and articulate the human cost of a devastating conflict. Something of this spirit was renewed at the centenary of these events. The King's Road project is one of several local expressions of this. Drawing, in particular, on earlier work by Ann Dean, Judy Sutton and Helen Little's meticulous research remembers fifteen lives tragically cut short as well as narrating a useful wider history of the street. The text is beautifully complemented with contemporary photographs and four moving poems by John Mole. It is especially good to see the inclusion of the three men whose names had already faded from local memory when the parish's Great War plaque and Memorial Hall were raised in the 1920s.

Rev Kenneth Padley, Vicar of St Michael's Church, St Albans

Historians talk airily about 'history from the street'. This is magnificent and poignant history from a very special street.

Sandy Walkington, County Councillor for St Albans (South) and a former president of the SAHAAS

I am delighted to see a memorial being installed on King's Road commemorating the brave service personnel who lost their lives during the Great War.

It's astonishing that this street in St Albans lost more men than many other streets in the city, yet there has been no record of their sacrifice. This memorial will be a lasting reminder of the human cost of war and of the fifteen men who tragically lost their lives.

I pay tribute to all King's Road residents who have done a fantastic job in finding an artist to design a memorial and in raising the funds to make it a reality.

This will be the first new street memorial in St Albans for some time and will ensure the lives of those who sacrificed so much will never be forgotten.

This book, too, will be a lasting record of the human cost of war and the fifteen men who tragically lost their lives.

Daisy Cooper, Member of Parliament for St Albans

This is a detailed, informative and impressively researched piece of local history. A moving tribute to the men who lost their lives in the Great War.

Sue Dyson, a resident of King's Road, St Albans

I was delighted when I read, in 'King's Road: for King and Country', the name of the house I had moved to in 2014. When my predecessor, John Edward Hunt and his parents, George and Jane, lived at No 3 it was known as Lily Cottage and I shall continue to call it that from now on.

I congratulate Judy and Helen on the immense amount of research they have done to bring this little road, tucked away in St Albans, back to life; to tell the 'backstory' of people who lived here over 100 years ago. It is a moving account, told with genuine pathos and heartfelt emotions, that makes today's residents proud to know what families went through during the Great War, in order to bring to those of us living now the freedoms we enjoy today.

When I moved to 3 King's Road it was the actual address that sparked my interest and made it one of the 'selling points' for me. I have often sung, at Christmastime, the carol, "We three kings", but never thought I would ever live in a house with that address. However, from now on, Number 3 will always be associated with Private John Edward Hunt, at one time of the Hertfordshire Regiment, one of the brave lads from King's Road, who died in the service of King and Country at the age 21 in 1918 and who, up until the time of his death, had lived at Lily Cottage.

Guy Marshall, a King's Road, St Albans, resident and a committee member of the Society of St Michael's and Kingsbury

About the compilers: Judy Sutton & Helen Little

Judy Sutton moved to King's Road St Albans with her husband in 1986. It was there that they raised their family. She has a keen interest in local and social history and, over the years, has enjoyed learning more about her street and its residents.

In 2018, when the country honoured those who had sacrificed their lives in the Great War, her thoughts turned to King's Road and the part it had played in this conflict. Who were the men and what were their stories?

This publication is a tribute to them and a reminder of how these ordinary men made extraordinary sacrifices.

A native of St Albans and life-long resident in the city, **Helen Little** found that becoming involved in the King's Road project has indulged two of her great loves: St Albans and genealogical research. One of Helen's great-grandfathers had been killed on the Somme, not knowing that he'd left a daughter.

Consequently, Helen is keen that the men of King's Road who died in the Great War are not forgotten. She believes that their stories should be told so that their memories can live on in the lives of their sons, daughters, nephews, nieces and wider family, along with those who are now connected, by residence, with their home city and street.

Contents

List of Illustrations

"From quiet homes and first beginning,
out to the undiscovered ends..."

Hilaire Belloc

Figure 1, St Michael's Church, St Albans c1910.
Photograph courtesy of Andy Lawrence.

Figure 2, St Michael's Church Great War Memorial, made from oak, erected c1922. A small rectangular board was added to the memorial in 2018 to include the names of five other men of the parish who had died in the Great War.

Introduction

Several years ago, I attended a display in St Michael's Church about their Great War memorial which had been organised by the local historian, Ann Dean. The names of those men from the parish who lost their lives in the Great War were listed and I was struck by the terrible loss of young life from our small street, King's Road. Fifteen lives were sacrificed from the 67 homes in our street. That may well be the largest loss of life – at least in percentage terms - from any street in St Albans. Of these 15 men, three were brothers. The youngest was 16 years old when he died and the oldest, 38.

These were ordinary men who did ordinary jobs. Their occupations included a gas worker, gamekeeper, cowman, boot factory worker, butcher's assistant, sawyer and postman. Many came from large extended families and were part of a close, mobile community. Parents, grandparents, brothers, sisters, uncles and aunts and cousins were frequently living nearby, either in King's Road or in the surrounding streets. Widowed grandparents, their children and grandchildren were often found together under one roof. It was not unusual to find eight people living together in one house. It was also not unusual to find that these families had lodgers. Houses were rented and families seemed to move frequently within a small radius.

It is clear that the war personally affected nearly every household since many men from King's Road served in the Great War and, remarkably, the majority survived. The Absent Voter list tells us that 58 servicemen from this street were away at war in 1918 (see Appendix 1). A rough calculation shows that more than three quarters of these men returned home.

More than 100 years later it is difficult to speculate on the impact of the Great War on the residents of King's Road. It's tempting to say that, for four years, life was consumed by tragedy but, prior to 1916, only one of its sons, William Hart, was lost. He was reported 'missing presumed dead' on 25th May 1915, possibly following the Second Battle of Ypres. He is commemorated on the Menin Gate.

After 1916, deaths mounted. William's brother, Henry Hart, and neighbour, Arthur Peters, lost their lives on 3rd September 1916 during the Battle of the Somme. This offensive claimed a total of one million men. Both Henry Hart and Arthur Peters have no known grave and are remembered on the Thiepval Memorial. Nineteen-year-old Fred Henry was wounded on 9th September 1916, quite possibly also at the Somme, and was taken to Boulogne military hospital where his parents were granted permission to visit him before he died. The fathers, Edward Atkins, Thomas Hunt and Alfred Foster, were killed in 1917, all leaving behind small sons. Edward Atkins and Thomas Hunt died in the summer of that year at Passchendaele, also known as the Third Battle of Ypres.

The remaining eight King's Road men died in the final year of the war. Many of them fell during the German Spring Offensive and the subsequent counter-attack. Particularly poignant are Charles Burridge who died on 9th May 1918 and his young nephew, John Hunt, who was lost less than three weeks later.

John has no known grave and is commemorated on the Soissons Memorial. Archie Faulder, who had served for more than three years, was killed in action 11 days before the war ended and is buried in a Commonwealth War Grave in a churchyard in Belgium. He had been home on leave earlier in the year. Sixteen-year-old Drummer boy, John Coleman, following in his two older soldier brothers' footsteps, had joined the Duke of Bedford's private band in Easter 1918. The influenza pandemic of 1918-19 claimed his life, along with that of 50 million people worldwide. John died on 24th October 1918 at Ampthill Red Cross hospital. He is buried in Soldier's Corner, Hatfield Road Cemetery, St Albans.

The Abbey parish of St Albans has ten street memorials dedicated to the memory of those who lost their lives in the Great War. These were erected in the first few years following the war. They are fashioned out of Portland stone and presented in a traditional tablet form. We believe that it is now time for King's Road, which is located in St Michael's parish, to have its own memorial using modern materials and a contemporary design. We chose to include on our memorial all those who died while serving their country in the Great War and whose family lived in King's Road during this time.

It is an idea that has certainly captured the imagination and support of many of our neighbours. Its ripples have spread further afield. We have been fortunate to have had offers of help and support from various groups and individuals including Jon Mein of the St Albans and Hertfordshire Architectural and

Archaeological Society (SAHAAS), County Councillor Sandy Walkington and Councillor Edgar Hill. Edgar has been instrumental in getting St Albans District Council to add our memorial to their existing street memorial portfolio.

We have also been extremely fortunate to have secured the help of artist Renato Niemis, who created the 'Counting the Cost' glass memorial at the Imperial War Museum at Duxford. He has designed a beautiful, subtle memorial made from Corten – a type of rusty metal – in the form of 'bricks' that represent the earth of the trenches and the ordinary nature of these men. It is also the same size as, and is symbolic of, the telegram these bereaved families would have received. At the time of writing our memorial has not yet been erected but our plans are moving forward.

We have been in touch with several of the relatives of these men and they have shared with us information they have including photos, letters and pictures of medals and graves. With the help of Gareth Hughes and Helen Little from the Herts at War group, along with Jon Mein of SAHAAS, we have now collated this information into booklet form.

During our research we came across a newspaper report in The Herts Advertiser of 6th April 1907, where we learn that the teenage condition is not such a recent phenomenon. These Edwardian lads also enjoyed hanging around in noisy, boisterous groups causing annoyance to the general public, just as some teenagers do today!

Under the headline 'The London Road Promenade' (see Appendix 2), it reports that William Hart (see page 30) and George Jeffs of King's Road as well as Arthur Peters of Blacksmiths Lane (see page 14), were part of a group of young men (The Herts Advertiser describes them as 'lads') who caused considerable public complaint by their anti-social behaviour, so much so that St Albans police felt compelled to act.

Head Constable Whitbread sent several police constables in plain clothes to patrol the Sunday promenade on London Road on 1st April, resulting in 11 cases being brought before the magistrates of either using bad language or obstructing the highway. Arthur Peters, of Blacksmiths Lane (later of King's Road) was fined six shillings for using bad language. William Hart and George Jeffs, both from King's Road were younger and received a caution. The report reads: 'The cases were brought as a warning to others in order to check this nuisance and render London Road a fair and proper place for people to walk up and down'.

Less than ten years later, both William Hart and Arthur Peters had lost their lives in the Great War.

The following pages tell the stories of these ordinary men and the part they played in the Great War. They are arranged according to their family house number.

Judy Sutton

Biographies of the Fallen of King's Road

WILLIAM THOMAS HUNT

WILLIAM THOMAS HUNT
Age 38, Gamekeeper

Lance Corporal 43489

4th Battalion, The King's (Liverpool Regiment)

Formally 3327,
The Hertfordshire Regiment

Killed in action
25th September 1917

William Thomas Hunt's parents lived at 2 King's Road, known as 'Fairleigh', at the time of his death.

William Thomas Hunt was born in 1879 in St Albans, the son of Joseph and Mary Ann Hunt (née Smith). He was one of 13 children, of whom seven survived to adulthood. His parents were also born in St Albans. He attended St Michael's School. His obituary in The Herts Advertiser of 20th October 1917 states that 'as a lad he was employed first by Mr C. Woollam as stable boy and, afterwards, by Mr Graham Fish, Oaklands, Hatfield-road as under-coachman'.

Figure 3, St Michael's main ('top') school, beside St Michael's Church.

In the 'Situations Wanted' section of the Somerset *Western Gazette* in February 1909, William is seeking work as a gamekeeper.

'Gamekeeper seeks situation as underkeeper or would take charge of beat. Understands pheasant and wild duck rearing. Good rabbit and vermin catcher. Age 28, height 5 ft 8 in, weight 11 stone. Good references from nobleman's estates. Single or married when suited. – W. Hunt, 2 King's Road, St Albans.'

William may well have placed similar notices around the country as, not long after 1909, he was working for Lord Derby at Knowsley Park near Liverpool and then for the Marquis de Castiga at Haskayne near Ormskirk. The 1911 census finds him lodging in Ormskirk working as a gamekeeper. He married Catherine Scarisbrick on 1st November 1911 and a son, Robert, was born in 1914. At the time of William's death, his wife was living at Twin Lodge, Scarisbrick, Ormskirk, Lancashire.

William Hunt joined the army on 26th June 1916 when he was 37 years of age. His obituary, titled 'A Real Hero's Death' states:

> 'An exceeding kind letter was received by the widow from Capt Herbert B. Tripp, in which he speaks most highly of the deceased soldier, and in the course of it he states, "It is with deepest sympathy that I am writing to tell you what a fearful loss your husband is to the battalion and especially to my company. I cannot possibly tell you how much we all appreciate the fine soldierly qualities of Corpl Hunt, who, though acting as a cook at the officers' mess at the time, took his rifle and helped us when we were being hard pressed by the enemy to beat off the attack. It was whilst he was firing at the approaching enemy that he was shot through the head by a stray bullet. He died immediately and was buried where he fell … your husband was undoubtedly one of the finest soldiers and certainly the best-liked man of the battalion. He died as fine a death as any man has in a fearful way - a real hero's death".'

William Hunt has no known grave and is commemorated on Tyne Cot Memorial, Zonnebeke, West-Vlaanderen, Belgium, Panel 31 to 162 and 162A and 163A. He is also remembered on the St Peter's Street and St Michael's Church memorial.

William's father, Joseph, was still living at 2 King's Road at the time of the 1939 register. He died in St Albans the following year.

Figure 4, Tyne Cot Memorial, Zonnebeke, West-Vlaanderen, Belgium. Photograph courtesy of CWGC.

On its website, The Commonwealth War Graves Commission (CWGC) describes the origins of the Tyne Cot Memorial.

'Tyne Cot Cemetery is in an area known as the Ypres Salient … Tyne Cot, or 'Tyne Cottage' was a barn which stood near the level crossing on the road from Passchendaele to Broodseinde. Around it were a number of German blockhouses … Many of those who fell at Passchendaele battlefields were buried here … After the Armistice, the cemetery was enlarged when graves from the battlefields of Passchendaele and Langemarck were brought here.'

JOHN EDWARD HUNT

JOHN EDWARD HUNT
Age 21

Private 292696

12/13th Battalion,
Northumberland Fusiliers

formerly 5488,
The Hertfordshire Regiment

Died 29th May 1918

John Edward Hunt's parents lived at 3 King's Road, known as Lily Cottage, at the time of his death.

John Edward Hunt was born in 1898 in St Michael's, the second son of George Albert Hunt, a farm labourer originally from Houghton Regis, and Jane (née Roberts). His grandparents, Alfred and Kezia Roberts, also lived in King's Road at number 15, known as Lanark Villa.

He was one of four children. The 1911 census describes him as a schoolboy living with his parents at 38 Portland Street.

By 1914-15 the family had moved to 3 King's Road. The Herts Advertiser, of 22nd April 1916, featured a picture of John alongside pictures of eleven of his uncles and cousins under the heading 'Our Patriotic Families'.

It describes how John's grandparents, Mr and Mrs Roberts of Lanark Villa, 15 King's Road, St Albans, 'are proud of their soldier family ... serving their King and Country' (see Appendix 3).

John Hunt's older brother, Albert Alfred, also served in the Great War as Gunner 37690 in the Royal Field Artillery. He died 8th March 1968 at 24 Hill Street, aged 73.

John's family remained in King's Road for many years.

His grandmother, Kezia, died in 1933 at 3 King's Road. His mother, Jane, was recorded as living at 3 King's Road in 1939, together with his younger brother, Arthur Cecil Hunt, a milk salesman, and Arthur's wife, Violet. Their daughter, Valerie, was born in 1941. Valerie states that she and her family continued living there until the death of her grandmother, Jane Hunt, in 1955.

The Hertfordshire Roll of Honour describes John Edward Hunt as having formerly been 5488, The Hertfordshire Regiment. He has no known grave and is commemorated on Soissons Memorial, Aisne, France.

John is also remembered on the St Michael's Church and St Peter's Street memorials.

Figure 5, Soissons Memorial, Aisne, France.
Photograph courtesy of CWGC.

The CWGC says of Soissons, 'The British Expeditionary Force crossed the Aisne in August 1914, a few kilometres west of Soissons and re-crossed it in September a few kilometres east. For the next three and a half years, this part of the front was held by French forces and the city remained within the range of German artillery. At the end of April 1918, five divisions of Commonwealth forces (IX Corps) were posted to the French 6th Army in this sector to rest and refit following the German offensives on the Somme and Lys. Here at the end of May, they found themselves facing the overwhelming German attack which, despite fierce opposition, pushed the Allies back across the Aisne to the Marne'.

ARTHUR WILLIAM PETERS

ARTHUR WILLIAM PETERS
Age 30, Sawyer

Private 27974

1st Battalion,
The Bedfordshire Regiment

Killed in action
3rd September 1916

Arthur William Peters' parents were living at 7 King's Road, known as 'Ivy Cottage', at the time of his death.

Arthur William Peters was born in St Albans in 1886, the son of Walter William and Ann Peters (née Stone). He was the eldest of seven children and attended Hatfield Road Elementary School.

On the 1901 census, aged 15, Arthur was working as a shoemaker and living with his family in 39 Fishpool Street. By 1911 the family had moved to 17 Blacksmiths Lane, St Michael's, where Arthur was working as a sawyer, an occupation he shared with his father and grandfather.

By 1914-15 the family were living at 7 King's Road.

His obituary in The Herts Advertiser states that, before enlisting 'he worked with his father for fifteen years in the service of the Earl of Verulam in the wood yard on the Gorhambury estate'.

Figure 6, Hatfield Road Elementary School, Empire Day 1909. Hatfield Road Elementary School was situated near St Peter's Church, behind the current Alban City school. The last of the school's buildings to be demolished was the Pemberton building in 2016.
Photograph courtesy of Ian Tonkin.

Arthur Peters joined The Bedfordshire Regiment on 29th March 1916 and his obituary states that he had only been 'in the trenches two or three days when he was killed'.

A £3 war gratuity was paid to his father, as Arthur's next of kin.

The Peters' extended family remained living in King's Road for several decades after Arthur's death.

A nephew, from 7 King's Road, also named Arthur Peters, served in the Second World War and survived.

Figure 7, Gorhambury House c1907.
Photograph courtesy of Andy Lawrence.

The 1939 register confirms that, at that time, Arthur's father, Walter, was living at 17 King's Road with his daughter, Violet, and Violet's husband, Harold Payne.

Arthur Peters has no known grave.

He is commemorated on the St Michael's Church and St Peter's Street memorials.

He is also commemorated on the Thiepval Memorial, Somme, France, Pier and Face 2C.

Figure 8, Thiepval Memorial, Somme, France.
Photograph courtesy of CWGC.

The CWGC says of Thiepval, 'The Memorial commemorates more than 72,000 men of British and South African forces who died in the Somme sector before 20th March 1918 and have no known grave, the majority of whom died during the Somme offensive of 1916. It is the largest Commonwealth memorial to the missing in the world.'

WILLIAM JENNINGS ASHBY

WILLIAM JENNINGS ASHBY
Age 23, Gas Worker

Private 36233

5th Battalion, Princess Charlotte of
Wales's (Royal Berkshire) Regiment

Formally 4824,
The Hertfordshire Regiment

Died of wounds
1st September 1918

William Jennings Ashby's mother, Mrs Saunders, was living at 8 King's Road at the time of his death.

William John Jennings Ashby was born in 1895 in Park Street, near St Albans, the son of Mary Ann Ashby.

In the 1891 and the 1901 censuses, his mother, Mary Ashby, was working as a domestic servant and housekeeper to Frederick Saunders. Frederick Saunders and Mary Ashby married in 1905 and William was named as the son of Frederick and Mary on the 1911 census.

His obituary in The Herts Advertiser, of 14th September 1918, states that, prior to enlisting, William 'was employed at the St Albans Gas Works and was educated at Park Street School'.

William Ashby enlisted in April 1915. In July 1917 he was drafted to the Western Front and took part in the severe fighting at the Battle of Arras, Ypres and St Julien, and was twice wounded. His obituary states that he 'died in hospital in Rouen on 1st September as the result of wounds received in action on 25th August.'

William Jennings Ashby is buried in St Sever cemetery extension Rouen, Seine-Maritime, France, Section R. Plot 11. Row 0. Grave 17. He is commemorated on the St Peter's Street memorial.

Figure 9, St Sever cemetery extension, Rouen, France.
Photograph courtesy of CWGC.

CHARLES EDWARD BURRIDGE

CHARLES EDWARD BURRIDGE

Age 34, Postman

Private G/2217

'B' Company, 8th Battalion,
The Royal Sussex Regiment

Killed in action
9th May 1918

Charles Edward Burridge's in-laws, Alfred and Kezia Roberts, were living at 15 King's Road, known as Lanark Villa, for several years until just before his death in 1918.

Charles Edward Burridge was born in 1883 in St Albans, the third of six children, to James and Louisa Burridge. His mother was originally from Liverpool and his father was from St Albans.

In 1901, the family were living at 113 Verulam Road and Charles was working as a postman, alongside his two older brothers.

He married Minnie Maud Roberts in 1906.

Minnie's large family were living at 15 King's Road before and during the First World War and her parents, Alfred and Kezia Roberts, were described by The Herts Advertiser in 1916 as one of 'Our Patriotic Families' who provided 12 family members (sons, sons-in-law and grandsons, including John Hunt of 3 King's Road) to serve in the First World War (see Appendix 3).

Charles joined-up at the beginning of the War and was killed some six months before the War's end.

The National Roll of the Great War 1914-1918 states that Charles Burridge 'volunteered in September 1914 and, in July of the following year, was sent to the Western Front, where he took part in the heavy fighting at Festubert, Loos, the Somme, Arras, Ypres and Cambrai.

'He was killed in action near Albert on 9th May 1918 and was entitled to the 1914-15 Star and the General Service and Victory Medals'.

Charles' granddaughter still has his medals today.

His final address was given as 6 Lower Dagnall Street.

Charles is buried in Warloy-Baillon Communal Cemetery Extension, Somme, France, Plot V111, Row G, Grave 3.

He is also remembered on the St Michael's Church and St Peter's Street memorials.

All of Charles' four brothers served in the First World War. Two of them survived.

Figure 10, Charles Burridge's Great War medals (from left): 1914 Star Medal; British War Medal 1914-1920; Allied Victory Medal 1914-1919. These were also known as the 'Pip, Squeak and Wilfred' medals - named after popular comic strip characters of the time.
Photograph courtesy of Janet Bates.

Charles and Minnie had three children, all boys. The youngest, George Richard, was born on 22nd July 1918, just two months after his father's death. Charles and Minnie's middle son, Edward, was lost during a sea crossing from Ceylon to Singapore in 1942.

Figure 11, A Memorial Plaque for Charles Edward Burridge.
Commonly known as 'The Dead Man's Penny', these were issued after
the Great War to the next-of-kin of all British and Empire service
personnel who were killed as a result of the war.

Photograph courtesy
of Janet Bates.

ARCHIE FAULDER

ARCHIE FAULDER
Age 20, Butcher's Assistant

Sergeant 202588

18th Battalion,
The Highland Light Infantry

Killed in action
31st October 1918

Archie Faulder's parents were living at 17 King's Road, also known as Salisbury Villa, at the time of his death, according to his obituary in The Herts Advertiser.

Archie William Faulder was born in 1898, in Redbourn, to George and Rose Ann Faulder. He was one of nine children. On the 1911 census, his father's occupation is described as 'horsebreaker' and the family are living at Salisbury Villa, King's Road. Before joining up, Archie worked for Mr T G Potten, a butcher in St Albans.

His obituary, printed in The Herts Advertiser, of 23rd November 1918, reported:

'News has reached Mr and Mrs G. Faulder, of Salisbury Villa, King's Road, St Albans that their fourth son, Sergt. Archie Faulder, aged 20, Highland Light Infantry, was killed in action on 31st October. He had been back from leave for about a fortnight when he met his death. He joined up in March 1915, in the Herts Regt and went to France in August 1917. He was home on special leave last December after bringing a German aeroplane down with a machine gun ... Mr and Mrs Faulder have four more sons serving, one of whom, Pte Herbert Faulder, 1st Herts, has been a prisoner of war in Germany since 22nd March 1918. Lieut J.V. Lindsey, in a sympathetic letter wrote stating: "He was one of the best Sergeants in the company and a fine soldier, always cheery, which went a long way to cheer those around him". The Reverend H.F. Toulmin C.F., in a lengthy and very kind letter wrote: "He was so manly and straightforward about his religion, and ever willing and anxious to help me in my work".'

Pierre Vandervelden, a Belgian war graves historian, writing on Ancestry UK, says, 'Archie signed up for the Army giving a false date of birth but the army found out he was only sixteen and sent him home. He returned to the army as soon as he was old enough'.

Archie is buried close to the East end of the Church in Outrijve Churchyard, Avelgem, West-Vlaanderen, Belgium. He is also remembered on the St Michael's Church and St Peter's Street memorials.

Figure 12, CWGC gravestone of Sergeant A Faulder,
in Outrijve churchyard, Belgium.
Photograph courtesy Pierre Vandervelden.

Archie's three brothers survived the Great War - including Herbert, who had been a prisoner of war.

Herbert went on to run a shop in Catherine Street. He lived in Hill Street and died in 1956, aged 61 years.

Two of Archie's nephews - sons of his brother Percy - fought and died in the Second World War. George William Faulder died on 12th February 1942 in Singapore and Archie Edward Faulder died on 10th June 1944 in Italy.

FOUR SOLDIER SONS.

The above photograph illustrates the patriotism of a St. Albans family. It shows four of the sons of Mr. and Mrs. George Faulder, of Salisbury Villa, King's-road, who have answered their country's call. Reading from left to right, they are Pte. Archie Faulder, 1st Herts Regt.; Pte. Percy Faulder, 1st Herts Regt.; and Pte. Herbert Faulder, 1st Herts Regt.; and, seated in front, Pte. Harry Faulder, of the Canadian Contingent. They are all in training in England at the present time. Pte. Percy Faulder, the eldest son, was in the Territorials before the war broke out and had completed his term, but readily re-enlisted for active service. He was employed as drayman by Messrs. Adey & White. Pte. Harry Faulder, who is the second son, was employed as a lad with Messrs. Stevens, grocers, of St. Albans, and later with Mr. C. Pearce, at Market Cross. He went to Canada in May, 1913, and joined the Canadian Contingent in Canada. The third son, Pte. Herbert Faulder, who enlisted twelve months ago, was formerly in the service of Messrs. Fletchers, Ltd., butchers; and Pte. Archie Faulder, the fourth son, was employed by Mr. T. G. Potton, butcher. He joined last May.

Figure 13, 'Four Solider Sons', The Herts Advertiser,
11th December 1915.

THE HART FAMILY

FOUR FIGHTING BROTHERS.

Reading from left to right: (1) Gunner Ernest Hart, with the R.F.A. in Egypt; (2) Pte. H. C. Hart, Manchester Regt., reported missing; (3) Pte. P. W. Hart, King's Royal Rifles, reported killed; (4) Sapper A. E. Hart, who has just sailed for the war area. These are four sons of Mr. and Mrs. George Hart, Hope Cottage, King's-road, St. Albans. Particulars of this patriotic family were given in last week's "Herts Advertiser."

Figure 14, Four Fighting Brothers, The Herts Advertiser,
14th October 1916.

The parents of William, Henry and Ernest Hart were living at Hope Cottage, King's Road, St Albans at the time of their sons' deaths.

There may be some confusion about the Hart family's address. Various records up to 1916 show the family living at number 21 King's Road. The obituary in The Herts Advertiser shows them living at Hope Cottage, which we understand to be number 23. In 1922, the Kelly's Directory records George Heart *(sic)* as living at 23 King's Road. The family may have moved from numbers 21 to 23 in 1916.

PHILIP WILLIAM HART

PHILIP WILLIAM HART
Age 23, Grocer

Private 10242

4th Battalion,
The King's Royal Rifle Corps

Killed in Action
25th May 1915

Philip William Hart (known as William) was the ninth of 13 children. He was born in St Albans in 1892 to Eliza (née Carrington) and George Hart, a gardener. The 1911 census describes William as a grocer living with his parents and seven of his siblings in King's Road.

The Herts Advertiser, of 7th October 1916, under the headline 'Two out of Four Taken' describes how William was reported missing on 25th May 1915:

> 'Nothing more was heard until about three months ago, when he was officially reported killed. A month ago his effects arrived home, and these included his "Soldier's Small Book", which bore the mark of a bayonet thrust

through the middle and a bullet mark through the corner. Three or four months before he was killed, he was invalided home with frost-bitten feet and enteric fever.'

William Hart is commemorated on the Menin Gate. He has no known grave. He is also remembered, together with his brothers, on the St Michael's Church and St Peter's Street memorials.

Figure 15, The Ypres Memorial (Menin Gate), Ypres, Belgium. Photograph courtesy of CWGC.

The CWGC says of the Menin Gate, 'The Ypres (Menin Gate) Memorial, often referred to simply as the Menin Gate, bears the names of 54,000 soldiers who died in Belgium and have no known grave. Between October 1914 and September 1918 hundreds of thousands of servicemen of the British Empire marched through the town of Ypres' Menin Gate on their way to the battlefields. The memorial now stands as a reminder of those who died who have no known grave and is perhaps one of the most well-known war memorials in the world ... Since 1928, the Last Post has been sounded every evening at 8pm under the memorial. Only during the Second World War was the ceremony interrupted.'

HENRY CHARLES HART

HENRY CHARLES HART
Age 26, Assistant Gardener

Private 26042

9th Battalion, The Royal Lancashire
Regiment

Died 3rd September 1916

Henry Charles Hart (known as Harry) was the seventh of 13 children. He was born in St Albans in 1890 to Eliza (née Carrington) and George Hart, a gardener. The 1911 census describes him as a railway engine cleaner, living with his parents and seven of his siblings in King's Road.

The Herts Advertiser, of 7th October 1916, under the headline 'Two out of Four Taken', describes how two of their sons, Henry Charles and Philip William were both reported missing:

> 'Mr and Mrs George Hart of Hope Cottage, King's Road, St Albans, have been officially informed that their third son, Private Henry Charles Hart (26), single, of the Manchester Regiment, has been missing since 3rd Sept.

Private Hart enlisted in February and went to the front in the latter part of June. He was assistant gardener with Mrs Gibson, Ashwell House, Verulam Road, St Albans'.

Henry Charles Hart has no known grave and is commemorated on the Thiepval Memorial. He is also remembered, with his brothers, on the St Michael's Church and St Peter's Street memorial.

The CWGC says of Thiepval, 'The Memorial commemorates more than 72,000 men of British and South African forces who died in the Somme sector before 20th March 1918 and have no known grave, the majority of whom died during the Somme offensive of 1916. It is the largest Commonwealth memorial to the missing in the world.'

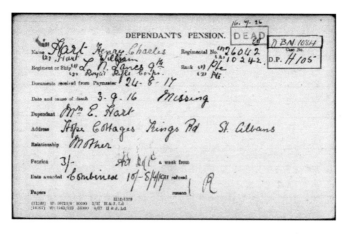

Figure 16, Henry Hart and [Philip] William Hart's Dependant Pension record. Reproduced with permission of the Western Front Association.

ERNEST HART

ERNEST HART
Age 35, Draper's Porter

Gunner 890313

20th Brigade,
The Royal Horse Artillery

Died in Palestine
4th July 1918

Ernest Hart was the fourth of 13 children. He was born in St Albans in 1888 to George, a gardener, and Eliza Hart. He married Rose Dimmock in 1906.

On the 1911 census he is described as working as a draper's porter, living in Harley Street (now known as Mount Pleasant), St Albans with his wife and two children, Ernest Frederick, born in 1907 and Mary Alice, born in 1909. His parents and seven of his brothers and sisters lived nearby in King's Road.

Ernest's obituary in The Herts Advertiser, under the headline 'Killed in Egypt', reports:

> 'Mrs E. Hart, of 34 Harley Street St Albans, has received the news from the War Office to the effect that her

husband Gnr. E. Hart, Herts RFA, was killed
(accidentally) in Egypt on 6th July 1918. Gnr. E. Hart
joined the Herts Regiment soon after the outbreak of
war and after a short *[period of]* training in England was
sent out to France. After being in France a few weeks,
he was sent out with a draft to Egypt and had seen
service in that part for nearly three years. He leaves a
widow and two children. Before enlisting Gnr. E. Hart
was employed by W.S. Green, of St Albans. Gnr. Hart
has had two brothers killed in the war and a younger
brother is still serving.'

The Commonwealth War Graves Commission contemporary
records document Ernest's date of death as 4th July rather than
6th July. Ernest Hart is buried in Ramleh War Cemetery, Israel
and Palestine (including Gaza), Section G, Grave 24. He is also
remembered with his brothers on the St Michael's Church and
St Peter's Street memorials.

The CWGC says of Ramleh War Cemetery in modern day Israel,
'The cemetery dates from the First World War, when Ramleh
(now Ramla) was occupied by the 1st Australian Light Horse
Brigade on 1st November 1917.

'Field Ambulances and, later, Casualty Clearing Stations, were
posted at Ramleh and Lydda from December 1917 onwards.
The cemetery was begun by the medical units, but some graves
were brought in later from the battlefields and from Latron,
Sarona and Wilhema Military and Indian Cemeteries.'

Figure 17, Ramleh War Cemetery, Israel.
Photograph courtesy of CWGC.

A great-nephew of the Hart brothers writes, 'There were six boys in total in the family and five went to war but only two came back. My grandfather was the youngest and was too young to join at the start of the war but, on his birthday (following the death of his closest brother), he went and signed-up. On hearing the news, his mother went to the conscription office and successfully demanded back the papers saying, "you're not taking another one of my sons."'

A fourth brother, Albert Hart, fought in the Great War and survived. In 1939 he was working as a railway engine driver and living in Dalton Street, St Albans.

JOHN GEORGE COLEMAN

JOHN GEORGE COLEMAN
Age 16 Drummer Boy

Drummer Boy to the Duke of
Bedford's Private Band

Died on 24th October 1918

John Coleman's parents were living at 25 King's Road, known as Brimscombe, at the time of his death.

John Coleman was born in 1902 in St Albans, the son of George and Leah Richardson Coleman (née Walker). He was one of six children.

On the 1911 census, John's father George is working as a boot and shoe repairer and the family is living at 25 King's Road.

The Herts Advertiser, under the headline 'Drummer J.G Coleman. Death from Pneumonia following Influenza', published his obituary on 9th November 1918:

'Drummer John George Coleman, Duke of Bedford's

Private Band, third son of Mr and Mrs Coleman, 'Brimscombe', King's Road, St Albans, died of pneumonia following influenza on 24th October at the Red Cross Hospital, Ampthill. He was sixteen years of age and joined up at Easter. He was at one time a pupil at the Abbey School and before enlisting was employed at Messrs Johnson's straw hat factory, Dagnall Street, St Albans'.

Figure 18, J G Coleman's gravestone, Soldiers' Corner, Hatfield Road Cemetery, St Albans.

Photograph courtesy of Herts at War.

John is buried in Soldiers' Corner at Hatfield Road Cemetery, St Albans. His grave was marked by a Commonwealth War Grave headstone. Many years later John's headstone was converted to a civilian stone, indicated by the left and right top corners of the headstone being stepped. He is also remembered on the St Michael's Church and St Peter's Street memorials.

John's older brothers, William and Edward, also served in the Great War and survived. John's parents were still living in King's Road in 1939.

Poem to Drummer John Coleman

Drummer John Coleman,

Eager, courageous,

Prepared for adventure

Not long out of school

Enlisted at Easter

Died in October

Too young to see action

His brief war ended

By bronchial pneumonia

Buried with honour

A short life cut shorter

But let us extend it

To go where he leads

With metrical drumbeat

With verse bugle sounding

As he would have had it

Not death but the glory

Of one last engagement

To grant him his wish.

by John Mole

ALFRED FOSTER

ALFRED FOSTER
Age 36, Bricklayer's Labourer

Private G/18717

1st Battalion, The Buffs
East Kent Regiment

Killed in action
26th March 1917

Alfred Foster's wife and son lived at 31 King's Road, known as Clapton Cottage, at the time of his death.

Alfred Foster was born in 1881 in St Albans, the son of Henry James, who worked in the Silk Mill, and Ellen Foster (née Waller). He was one of seven children. He married Martha Figg in 1906 and they had one son, Alfred Alban Foster, who was born on 17th May 1907. The 1911 census places them at King's Road, in Clapton Cottage. Alfred was a bricklayer's labourer with builders Messrs Miskin and Sons before he joined the army.

Figure 19, St Michael's Infants ('Bottom') School, St Michael's Street.
Photograph courtesy of Ricky Barnett.

His obituary in The Herts Advertiser, of 21st April 1917, states:

'He was a St Michael's boy, was educated at St
Michael's School and before his marriage eleven years
ago, took a great interest in football and was a former
member of St Michael's and Abbey teams. He was a
member of the Lord Bacon Lodge of Oddfellows. The
following letter from his Adjutant has been received by
the widow: "In the Field, 28th March. Mrs Foster, I
deeply regret having to inform you of the death of your
husband, who was killed in action on 26th March. His
comrades sorely miss him, for he was always cheerful
and ever ready to help, and many are the kindly acts he
performed which gained their love. He was an excellent

soldier, willing and obedient, faithful in the discharge of his duties and trusted by all his officers. The Commanding Officer, the commissioned and non-commissioned officers and men of the battalion tender you their sincere sympathy in your sad bereavement. - W.B.BIRRELL, Captain and Adjutant.'''

Alfred Foster is buried in Maroc British Cemetery, Grenay, Pas de Calais, France, Plot 1, Row P, Grave 22. He is also commemorated on the St Michael's Church and St Peter's Street memorials. The CWGC says of Maroc British Cemetery, Grenay, 'The cemetery was begun by French troops in August 1915, but it was first used as a Commonwealth cemetery by the 4th (London) Division in January 1916. During the greater part of the War it was a front-line cemetery used by fighting units and field ambulances and protected from German observation by a slight rise in the ground'.

Alfred's son, Alban, placed an 'in memoriam' to his father in 1922 in The Herts Advertiser: 'He nobly fought. He did his best. Grant him, oh Lord, eternal rest. From Alban.'

FOSTER — In loving memory of my dear Dad, Pte. Alfred Foster, 1st Buffs, who was killed in action in France, March 26th, 1917.
He nobly fought. He did his best.
Grant him, oh Lord, eternal rest.
From ALBAN.

Figure 20, Alfred Foster, 'In Memoriam'.

Four Foster brothers served in the Great War and only one, William, returned.

Alfred's brother Edward Foster, a silk mill worker from 14

Albert Street, served with the Essex Regiment and died on 22nd March 1918, aged 35. He has no known grave and is commemorated on the Arras Memorial, Pas de Calais, France. He is also remembered on the Albert Street Abbey parish memorial and, with his two brothers, on the St Peter's Street memorial.

Alfred's brother, Walter, died two weeks after Edward on 6th April 1918, aged 29. Before enlisting with the 6th Battalion of

The Bedfordshire Regiment, he was living with his parents and sister at 29 Fishpool Street and was working at Vyse's straw-hat factory. He is buried at Gommecourt British Cemetery No 2, Hebuterne, Pas de Calais, France. He is also remembered on the Fishpool Street Abbey parish memorial, the Vyse's hat factory memorial in Ridgmont Road, St Albans, and, with his two brothers, on the St Peter's Street memorial.

FOUR MORE SOLDIER BROTHERS.

ONE KILLED AND ONE WOUNDED.

Above we reproduce another quartette of soldier-brothers. They are, Pte. Alfred Foster, killed; Pte. William Foster; Pte. Edward Foster; Corpl. Walter Foster, wounded. Prior to enlistment Ptes. Edward and William Foster were employed at the Silk Mill, St. Albans, and Walter at Messrs. Vyse's straw hat factory. Edward was transferred to the Essex Regt. and went to France on Oct. 11th, 1916, William is in the Beds Regt. and stationed in England, whilst Walter was wounded on April 11th, 1917, a fact which was communicated to his sister on Sunday. They are sons of Mr. and Mrs. H. J. Foster, of 29, Fishpool-street, St. Albans.

Private Alfred Foster, 1st Battn Buffs Regt., No. 31, King's-road, St. Albans, who was killed in France on March 26th (as reported in our last issue), was a bricklayer's labourer with Messrs. Miskin & Sons, builders, before he joined the Army ten months ago. He leaves a widow and one little boy aged ten. He was a St. Michael's boy, was educated at St. Michael's School, and before his marriage eleven years ago took a great interest in football and was a former member of the St. Michael's and Abbey teams. He was a member of the Lord Bacon Lodge of Oddfellows. The following letter from his Adjutant has been received by the widow:— "In the Field, March 28th. Mrs. Foster,—I deeply regret having to inform you of the death of your husband, who was killed in action on March 26th. His comrades sorely miss him, for he was always cheerful and ever ready to help, and many are the kindly acts he performed which gained their love. He was an excellent soldier, willing and obedient, faithful in the discharge of his duties and trusted by all his officers. The Commanding Officer, the commissioned, non-commissioned officers and men of the battalion tender you their sincere sympathy in your sad bereavement.—W. B. BIRRELL, Captain and Adjutant."

Figure 21, Four More Soldier Brothers, The Herts Advertiser, 21st April 1917.

EDWARD RICHARD JAMES ATKINS

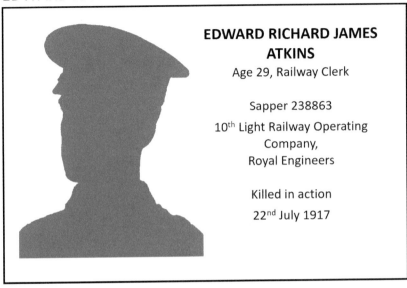

EDWARD RICHARD JAMES ATKINS

Age 29, Railway Clerk

Sapper 238863

10th Light Railway Operating Company,
Royal Engineers

Killed in action
22nd July 1917

Edward Richard James Atkins' wife and parents-in-law were living at 39 King's Road, known as 'Haybury Cottage', at the time of his death.

Edward Atkins was born in Northampton in 1888, the son of George Edward and Clara Elizabeth Atkins.

He moved to St Albans, working as a railway clerk, and lived as a lodger of Mr and Mrs Rance at Haybury Cottage, King's Road, in 1911. He married their daughter, Caroline, a straw-hat machinist, in 1913 in St Albans. They had one son, Gordon, born on 5th April 1915 in Croydon.

The Commonwealth War Graves Commission (CWGC) describes the address of Edward's wife, Caroline, as 39 King's Road at the time of his death.

He is buried at Canada Farm Cemetery, Ypres, West-Vlaanderen, Belgium, Plot 1. Row F. Grave 24. Carved on his stone are the words 'Beloved husband of Caroline Atkins. Gone but not forgotten'.

Figure 22, Canada Farm Cemetery, Ypres, West-Vlaanderen, Belgium. Photograph courtesy of CWGC.

Edward Atkins is commemorated on the St Michael's Church and the St Peter's Street memorials.

The CWGC says of the Canada Farm Cemetery, 'Canada Farm Cemetery took its name from a farmhouse used as a dressing station during the 1917 Allied offensive on this front. Most of the burials are of men who died at the dressing station between June and October 1917. There are now 907 First World War burials in the cemetery.'

Caroline did not re-marry. She and her son, Gordon, were listed  as living together at 53 The Crofts, on the 1939 St Albans register. Gordon served in the RAF in the Second World War and died in service in a drowning accident in 1944, aged 28.

His mother's memorial stone is placed at the foot of his grave in Hatfield Road Cemetery, St Albans.

AC1 G. Atkins.

Figure 23, Gordon Atkins, the son of Edward and Caroline.

Poem to Sapper Edward Atkins

Sapper Edward Atkins, you were the man needed

To mend the track, to keep the railway running.

Often under fire, you carried out your task,

A sack of tools strapped to your back, finding the right one

For the job in hand. Thanks to you

The wounded made it safely to a hospital

Behind the lines and new recruits were carried

To the Front. You understood complexities of wire

And broken sleepers, how to fix the trucks

And carriages, to couple them to engines

You had thoroughly checked over. All this

In the face of imminent attack, singing perhaps

With comrades 'When this bloody war is over'

As it was for you before it ended, as we honour now

More than a name, a full life not to be forgotten.

By John Mole

GEORGE EDWARD HOWARD

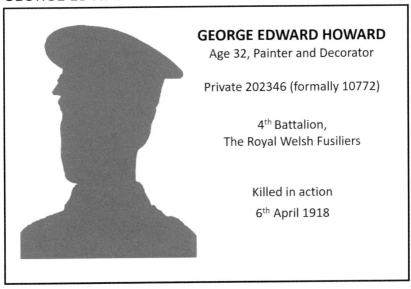

GEORGE EDWARD HOWARD
Age 32, Painter and Decorator

Private 202346 (formally 10772)

4th Battalion,
The Royal Welsh Fusiliers

Killed in action
6th April 1918

George Edward Howard's mother was living at 43 King's Road, known as 'Myrtledene', at the time of his death.

George Edward Howard was born in 1886 in St Albans, the eldest son of Mark and Annie Howard.

He was educated at the St Albans Abbey National School - and his obituary described him as 'the best writer in the school'.

George's father died in 1894, leaving his mother to support five children. By the 1901 census, his mother, Annie, had remarried - to Alfred Spicer - and the whole family of ten were living at 42 Fishpool Street, with everybody being surnamed Spicer. George's occupation was given as silversmith.

By 1911, eight of the family, including George's grandfather, were living at 43 King's Road. A distinction is made on this census between families and George is named as a 'Howard' and is described as a stepson. His occupation was given as brass finisher, working at a chronometer manufacturer.

George was killed in action on 6th April 1918 at the Somme, France.

Figure 24, The St Albans Abbey National Boys School, Spicer Street.

George's obituary in The Herts Advertiser of 11th May 1918 states:

> 'Pte George Edward Howard age 32, of the Royal Welsh Fusiliers, eldest son of the late Mr Mark Howard and of Mrs Howard, 'Myrtledene' King's Road, St Albans, was killed on 6th April, whilst in action with his regiment in France and was home on leave last November. He was educated at the Abbey School during the period of Mr Wilton Hall's headmastership and was regarded as the best writer in the school. Before joining the Army he was employed with Mr Watkins, Fishpool Street, painter and decorator.
>
> Mrs Howard *[by this time, Mrs Spicer]* has two other sons in the Colours, namely Corpl Samuel Howard, age 27, who is with the Military Mounted Police in Salonica and Lance Corpl Charles Howard *[really, George's half-brother, Charles Spicer]*, age 19, who is in the Norfolk Regiment.'

George Howard is remembered on the Pozieres Memorial and commemorated on the St Peter's Street memorial.

Figure 25, Pozieres Memorial, Ovillers-la-Boisselle, France.
Photograph courtesy of CWGC.

A pension of six shillings a week was awarded to his mother on 21st November 1918, by which time she had moved to 22 Queen Street.

George's younger half-brother, Charles Henry Spicer, who also served in the Norfolk Regiment during the Great War, married Florence Dugdale in 1926 and remained in St Albans until at least 1939. He worked as a male nurse.

The CWGC says of the Pozieres memorial, 'The Pozieres Memorial relates to the period of crisis in March and April 1918 when the Allied Fifth Army was driven back by overwhelming numbers across the former Somme battlefields, and the months that followed before the Advance to Victory, which began on 8th August 1918. The Memorial commemorates over 14,000 casualties of the United Kingdom and 300 of the South

African Forces who have no known grave and who died on the Somme from 21st March to 7th August 1918.'

*Figure 26, George Howard's Dependant Pension record.
Reproduced with permission of the Western Front Association.*

Poem to Private George Howard

Private George Edward Howard
of the Royal Welsh Fusiliers,
painter, silversmith, brass finisher,
a life as sure of its direction
as each of the chronometers
he touched, lover of precise
measurement and language,
man of skill and craft, worthy
of all due respect.
                    Respected too
and held in high regard as his school's
best writer, he would have admired
that telling phrase 'so densely
sown with sacrifice' once written
of the Somme whose memorial
at Pozieres records his name
as just one sacrificial seed.
                    Here now at home
we remember him and still give thanks
for his gift of the peace that flowered
into our nation's growth, and celebrate
the life he gave, a precious legacy
of service, hope and fellowship
never to be forgotten or betrayed.

By John Mole

PERCY WILLIAM COX

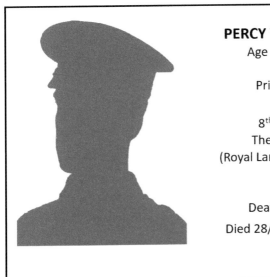

PERCY WILLIAM COX
Age 26, Cowman

Private 28431

8th Battalion,
The King's Own
(Royal Lancaster Regiment)

Death Presumed
Died 28/29th March 1918

Percy Cox's wife and, possibly, his parents were living at 55 King's Road at the time of his death.

Percy William Cox was born in 1891 in Graveley, Herts, the son of William and Amelia Cox (née Aldridge). He was one of eight children. According to the 1911 census, Percy was working as a cowman and living with his family at Shafford Cottages, St Albans.

He enlisted on 9th November 1915 in the Royal Lancashire Regiment and gave his address as 55 King's Road. He served for some months before returning home to work as a cowman and miller for Mrs Hammond of St Germain's Farm, St Michael's. The St Albans military service tribunal was told, in December

1916, that Mrs Hammond was planning to sell her farms and needed her farm hands until such time as this occurred. Percy was granted exemption from conscription until April 1917, when he returned to the Front. He married Alice Mary Tredgett on 27th October 1917 in St Albans.

Figure 27, Lifting the hay. Believed to be St Germain's farm c1905. Photograph courtesy of SAHAAS.

His army service record states 'death assumed' by War Office 'on lapse of time having occurred on or since 28th /29th March 1918'.

Alice was awarded a weekly pension of 13s 9d for a year.

Percy was commemorated on the Arras Memorial at Faubourg-D'Amiens Cemetery, Arras. He is also remembered on the St Michael's Church and St Peter's Street memorials.

Figure 28, Arras Memorial at Fauough-D'Amiens Cemetery, Arras, France.
Photograph courtesy of CWGC.

The CWGC says of the Arras memorial, 'The memorial commemorates almost 35,000 servicemen from the United Kingdom, South Africa and New Zealand who died in the Arras sector between the spring of 1916 and 7th August 1918, the eve of the Advance to Victory, and have no known grave. The most conspicuous events of this period were the Arras offensive of April-May 1917, and the German attack in the spring of 1918.'

Percy's younger brother, Ernest Cyril Cox, also served in the Great War and survived. On the 1939 Register Percy's mother, Amelia, was still living at 55 King's Road with Percy's brother, Ernest, a builder's labourer, and Ernest's wife, Margaret.

FERDINAND HAMMOND HENRY

FERDINAND HAMMOND HENRY

Age 19, Boot Factory Worker

Private 39576

8th Battalion,
The Gloucestershire Regiment

Died of wounds
12th October 1916

Ferdinand (known as Fred) Henry's parents were living at 61 King's Road at the time of his death.

Fred Henry was born about 1898 in Brixton London, the son of Ferdinand and Mary Ann Henry.

He was one of three children. In the 1911 census, his parents are described as licensed victuallers living at The Green Dragon in London Colney.

By 1911 Fred only had one sibling surviving, a sister called Ellen Gertrude. Fred's obituary in The Herts Advertiser of 4th November 1916 states:

Figure 29, Fred Henry (third from left in the back row peeping through posts) outside his family's pub, The Green Dragon at London Colney c1912.
Photograph courtesy of the London Colney Local History Society.

'Mr F. Henry of 61, King's Road St Albans, has received an official announcement that his only son, Pte Frederick *(sic)* Herts Regiment, attached Gloucesters, has died from wounds received in action. Deceased, who was 19 years of age, joined the Army in April of last year, and went out to France on 7th May last. On 7th September he was wounded in the head and was sent to a military hospital at Boulogne. Towards the end of September Mr and Mrs Henry obtained permission of the War Office and a pass to visit their son at Boulogne, an opportunity they greatly appreciated. The young fellow died a fortnight later, on 12th October. Before enlisting, the deceased was employed by Messrs Lee and Son, boot factory, St Albans. Formerly he was a member of the London Colney Church Lads' Brigade'.

In a letter that Fred sent home to his Aunt Annie, dated 2nd June, he writes:

'Dear Aunt Annie,

'Just a few lines to let you know that I am in the pink hoping you are the same. Well, Aunt, I dare say you know that I have been in France a month now and I don't think much of it. We are just behind the line in a small village … we have to load and unload trucks and make hurdles so there is plenty of work to do. We have to work Sundays and all so we don't have much time to ourselfs. It makes you laugh to hear the French people talk because you can not understand a thing they say. Well, Aunt, I have had a letter from mother and it says that she has had her old complaint again. I hope she can soon get rid of it, but I expect she is worrying about me that is what is making her bad. Remember me to Granny and Uncle Dave. Hoping they are in the best of health. Well, I don't think there is anything more to say. I hope to see you all after the war.

'From your loving nephew Fred'

Fred died of wounds and is buried at Boulogne Eastern Cemetery, Pas de Calais. He is also remembered on St Peter's Street, St Michael's Church and Lee's Boot factory memorials.

Fred's parents remained living in King's Road for many years after his death.

The CWGC says of Boulogne Eastern Cemetery, 'Boulogne was one of the three base ports most extensively used by the Commonwealth armies on the Western Front throughout the First World War.

It was closed and cleared on 27th August 1914 when the Allies were forced to fall back ahead of the German advance, but was opened again in October and, from that month to the end of the war, Boulogne and Wimereux formed one of the chief hospital areas.

Until June 1918, the dead from the hospitals at Boulogne itself were buried in the Cimetiere de L'Est, one of the town cemeteries, the Commonwealth graves forming a long, narrow strip along the right-hand edge of the cemetery'.

Figure 30, The gravestone of Private F Henry, in Boulogne Eastern Cemetery, France.

Photograph courtesy of Ros Trent.

IN THE PINK

Private Fred Henry,
just 19, first time abroad
and writing home
from his post in France,
wants all the family to know
he's 'in the pink',
gives tender reassurance
to his ailing mother
that all is well
with plenty of work to do
and the companionship
of fellow conscripts
though like them he's amazed
to hear the locals talking
in an unfamiliar language:
'We can't understand
a single word they say.
I've been here a month now
and I don't think much of it!'

Bending to his appointed task
of loading and unloading trucks
and of making hurdles,
safe behind the lines, he writes
to his aunt 'I hope to see you all

after the war', but all too soon
it's his mother and father alone
who see him, journeying to Boulogne,
permitted by an official pass
to visit him in hospital,
to comfort him and say Goodbye.

No longer in the pink
but dead of head wounds,
Fred Henry – first time abroad,
never to come home
now laid to rest in foreign soil.
Remember him, rather, as he is
in this poignant photograph
of a gathering outside the family pub,
not grown old, and peeping cheerily
through posts on the porch
as if at the man he may yet become
whose secrets are now his to keep.

By John Mole

Figure 31, The St Albans' Civic War Memorial dedication, 1921 – from the SAHAAS Arthur Allen collection.

History

There is evidence of human activity at least as far back as Roman times under King's Road and its surrounding streets.

This area is understood to be located on the site of a Roman cemetery. Many cremation urns and pottery fragments thought to be Roman were revealed during excavations made for drainage works c1885 in Mud Lane (now the western part of Mount Pleasant). When Kingsbury Avenue was being cut through, in early 1900, several Roman burials and two Roman coins were found.

The Lawns in Mount Pleasant was built in 1960 on the site of what the archaeologist, I E Anthony, described as 'slum clearance'. During construction, a large amount of material was excavated including three sides of a masonry building, two wells containing human and dog bones, and a large amount of Roman pottery.

A piece of Roman cremation pot was found during work carried out some years ago by the Gas Board outside number 21 King's Road. During the same works several Roman and medieval pottery fragments were found in a trench outside 57 King's Road.

Since Victorian times it has been understood that the Saxon settlement called Kingsbury was located on a raised area of land between Fishpool Street to the south, Verulam Road to the north and Branch Road to the west. This included the present-day King's Road within its boundary. However, this view has not been confirmed by archaeology. Niblett and Thompson in 'Alban's Buried Towns' (2005) conclude that this Saxon settlement is much more likely to have been located at the site of Roman Verulamium where buildings, materials and a water source from the River Ver would have been present.

Interestingly, a ditch of unknown date was identified in 1992 in the back garden of number 49 King's Road. It is not known if it is a section of medieval boundary, a Saxon defence or even Roman. It may be part of a much larger ditch (also undated) located behind Hill Street abutting the New England Field ('the Brickie' playing field) which follows the line of the medieval borough boundary.

The area on which King's Road was built remained as meadow land for several centuries. On the 1799 St Michael's parish map, the field that occupied this land was LXXI number 1. It was owned by Mr Jones and occupied by Mr Wellingham, and was three acres, two rods and five perches of meadow.

John Wellingham was a tanner, a local occupation that dated from the medieval period and he was probably the last of his trade in Fishpool Street. He was also a Turnpike Trust trustee. To qualify for this unpaid but very prestigious position potential trustees were required, by the 1791 St Albans Turnpike Trust Act, to possess a yearly income of at least one hundred pounds. He lived at Bell Meadow (now number 137) Fishpool Street at the site of his tanyard. He may well have used the 'King's Road meadow' on which to graze his horses.

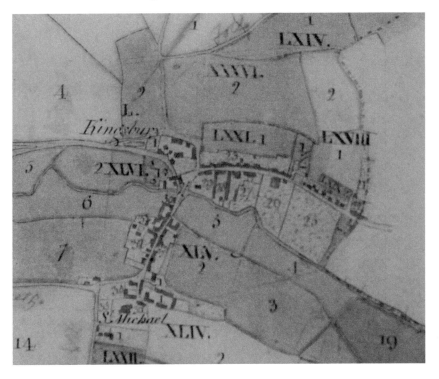

Figure 32, St Michael's Parish map, 1799. Reproduced by permission of the Vicar and Church Wardens of St Michael's Church, St Albans.

By the 19th century the land now occupied by King's Road was thought to be known as Black Lion Mead. It was used by successive tenants of the Black Lion Public House in Fishpool Street as cow pasture.

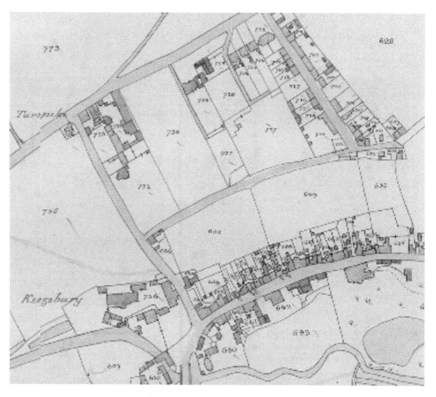

Figure 33, St Michael's Tithe map of 1843. Reproduced with permission of Hertfordshire Archives and Local Studies (HALS).

The St Michael's Tithe map of 1843 shows the site of King's Road as two parcels of land: 688 and 689 (please note that the numbering is slightly indistinct in the map). The reference book that accompanies this map (the 'tithe award') tells us:

688: owner Thomas Donne, occupier Henry Goodspeed, meadow, 1 acre, 2 rods 23 perches

689: owner Thomas Donne, occupier Henry Goodspeed, meadow, 1 acre, 3 rods and 38 perches

Henry Goodspeed was the occupier of the Black Lion from c1821 until his death in April 1863.

The 1861 census for The Black Lion Inn describes Henry as a cow keeper, aged 72, living with wife, Sarah, a dairywoman aged 74. Also living with him were his son William, William's wife Elizabeth and two (male) lodgers. By the 1871 census, The Black Lion Inn and dairy herd had been passed to William (Henry's son). His wife, Elizabeth's occupation was described as 'dairymaid'.

The herd comprised no more than 16 cows. These were milked in barns at the back of The Black Lion. They produced some 12 gallons of milk a day. The milk was carried down Fishpool Street with a yoke, in pails, and served with a ladle into a customer's own jug.

After Henry's death, members of the Goodspeed family were publicans at The Black Lion until 1879.

The oldest house in King's Road, called St Michael's Cottage, was thought to have been built in the 17th century. It lies

Figure 34, Black Lion corner. Waiting for King George V to pass on his way to Gorhambury to review the troops, 1914. Reproduced with permission of HALS.

between King's Road and Fishpool Street, built on land owned by 172 Fishpool Street.

It is located behind numbers 10 and 12 King's Road. It was built as two farm labourers' cottages with access from Fishpool Street. It is not known when the cottages were made into one dwelling but it may not have been long after Mary Emily Higgs bought them, along with 172 Fishpool Street and its surrounding yards and gardens, in 1901. Once King's Road was

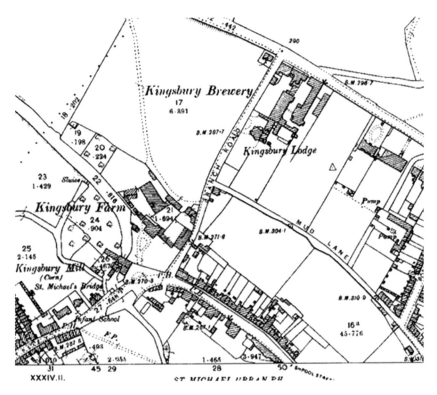

Figure 35, OS map c1897 (part) – see also Figure 36.
Map courtesy of SAHAAS.

built, a path was cut through to St Michael's Cottage creating rear access. It appears that, from this time, the cottage was listed as being part of King's Road.

In approximately 1970 the path from St Michael's Cottage to Fishpool Street was walled off, thus severing its connection to Fishpool Street.

Figure 36, OS map c1897 (part) – see also Figure 35.
Map courtesy of SAHAAS.

Kelly's Directory for 1903 lists King's Road but without any residents.

It seems that, from around that date, the street was laid down and the land divided into building plots which were sold to various builders.

Building started at the west end of the street in 1904 and was mostly completed by 1913.

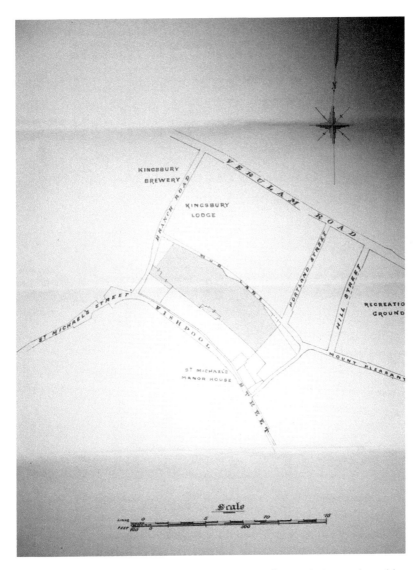

Figure 37, Site of King's Road, outlined in pink, 1903. Reproduced by courtesy of Neil and Rachel Robertson.

The 1903 map on the previous page outlines the site on which number 20 King's Road was built.

The area which will be King's Road is outlined in pink. The land was sold by Horace Slade, a straw-hat manufacturer, of Victoria Street, St Albans, to the house builder, William Butler, of 80 Fishpool Street.

Horace Slade was a leading local property developer of the time and twice mayor of St Albans.

This plot cost £32 and was described as 'Lot 80 of the Kingsbury Estate' in the contract of sale.

Figure 38, Mayor Horace Slade, straw-hat manufacturer, property developer and Mayor of St Albans 1904 and 1913-14.
Photograph courtesy of St Albans Museums.

*Figure 39, VE Day 1945 in King's Road. William Butler, then aged 88,
is shown at the rear of the picture.*

William Butler moved into number 20 King's Road and
continued living there with his family for many years.

Not all St Albans developers were as successful as Horace
Slade. The Herts Advertiser, of Saturday 26th May 1906, reports
that George Edward Archer, a builder, attended the St Albans
Bankruptcy court owing £338 10 shillings and 9 pence, £20 of
which he owed to Mr Slade. He had commenced trade as a
speculative builder in 1902 using his own savings accrued while
working as a journeyman carpenter, earning nine pence an
hour. He built one or two houses at a time, two of which were
built in King's Road, and then sold them to fund further
building. Sadly, he over stretched himself in the difficult

economic conditions of the day and his property business came crashing down in 1906.

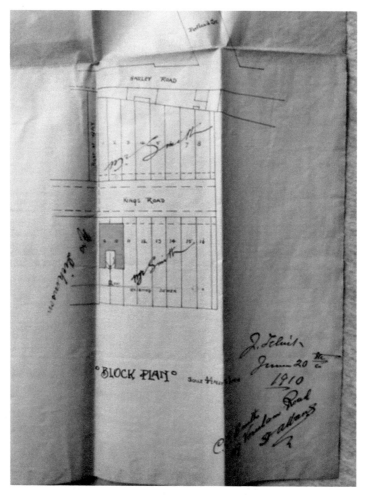

Figure 40, 1910 map of the site of land at the east end of King's Road sold to C C Smith of 147 Verulam Road. The map is reproduced courtesy of Chris and Jan Saunders.

The map on the previous page outlines the plot of land in King's Road that Cecil Cannon Smith bought in 1910. These plans are for 16 houses but 17 were built, probably because the houses on the north side were built with no alleyways.

The 1911 census shows Cecil Cannon Smith living with his wife, Fannie, and her parents in 147 Verulam Road. His occupation was described as straw-hat blocker. This was a period that saw St Albans expand rapidly and house building was often funded by small, speculative builders - of which Cecil Smith was one.

Cecil Smith moved into 58 King's Road soon after, naming his house, Cannonville. Cecil's employer, Horace Slade, the straw-hat manufacturer, made three successful applications between 1916 and 1917 for Cecil to be exempt from conscription. Cecil was finally called up in September 1917 at the age of 41. He served in the Great War and survived. Fannie died in 1941 and Cecil remained living at number 58 until his death in 1955.

Figure 41, Advertisements of houses to let in King's Road, from The Herts Advertiser in 1906 and 1907 respectively.

According to Valerie Allen, a niece of John Hunt (see page 11), who grew up in 3 King's Road, this eastern end of the street remained unadopted until at least the mid-1950s.

Joan Stanley, the niece of Fred Henry (see page 57), grew up in Fleetville in the 1930s and '40s. She remembers walking along

Mount Pleasant, on her way to visit her grandmother at 61 King's Road. She describes passing a house with a garden full of vegetables located just behind her grandmother's house at the north-east end of King's Road. A very friendly man called Mr Bunyan lived there. It appears that the two houses on Mount Pleasant behind King's Road were demolished at some point after the late 1930s and Mount Pleasant was widened.

The section of Mount Pleasant from Branch Road to just beyond Portland Street was originally named Mud Lane. It was given the more dignified name of Harley Street in the 1900s and included as part of Mount Pleasant sometime after 1923.

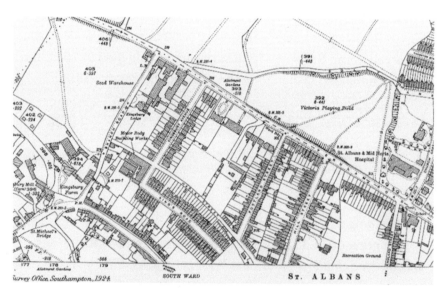

Figure 42, OS Map of St Albans, King's Road area in 1924. It is reproduced by courtesy of SAHAAS.

The builders bought their plots individually and in groups. This has resulted in an attractive variety of architectural styles applied to mainly terraced houses.

Some that were built in groups have the name of the terrace in a sandstone plaque in the middle of the row. Sadly, only one, Cranleigh Cottages on the south side of the street, is still legible. Houses were originally named rather than numbered.

The houses in King's Road were all planned to have a defined building line. This was six feet from the pavement to the front door irrespective of whether the houses had steps or not. This results in a clear sight line where one can see from one end of the street to the other.

Originally all the windows would have been of the sash type and the roofs tiled with slate. Some of the houses have porches, either wooden or brick.

Any gates are likely to have been of iron but no original ones have survived. Perhaps they were donated to the 'Saucepan to Spitfire campaign' that was launched in 1940 to provide aluminium and iron for the war effort.

The brickwork of the houses is predominantly red brick but Luton grey bricks have also been used, creating a contrast. The road is edged with attractive light blue granite sets and the pavement is made of the distinctive Staffordshire blue.

Figure 43, King's Road, 2020.
Photograph courtesy of Paul Peters.

Four houses were added to King's Road many years after the original development.

Nos 18A and 18B were built in 1959 on the site of an orchard owned by Mr William Henry Aldridge, located at the back of his bakery at 160 Fishpool Street. His daughter, Gladys Cooper, brought up her family in 18B and remained living there until her death in 2014.

Number 20A was completed in 2011.

A plot of land was left empty between numbers 11 and 13 for nearly 100 years. It is understood that the builder of number 13 ran out of funds and could not afford to build the house next door. This plot remained a green space until number 13 was extended in the 1990s.

Number 60 was built in 2009 on land belonging to Bank House, 122 Fishpool Street. This land was used as tennis courts in the 1950s.

The trees lining the pavement were added by the council in the 1960s at the request of the local residents, led by Edna Hames from number 53.

They were replaced in the early 2000s when their roots started lifting the pavements.

On the site of Gonnerston there was a photographic works and motor building works at the turn of the 20th century.

Cyril Pollock, who grew up in number 51 King's Road more than 100 years ago, remembered his mother working in a factory on this site making soldiers' uniforms during the Great War.

The Gonnerston houses were built in 1963 by Herbert Cox and Gear and are locally listed. The origin of the name comes from a medieval boundary marker called the 'Gonnerstone'. This is thought to be the puddingstone outside Kingsbury Manor house at the junction of St Michael's Street and Fishpool Street.

Kingsbury Avenue was built on a parcel of land also owned by Horace Slade known as the Kingsbury Brewery 'Paddock'. It was cut through in approximately 1908 and finished by 1920.

Figure 44, St Michael's Village c1910.
Photograph courtesy of Andy Lawrence.

1911 Census

*[**A note of caution:** When reading the 1911 census, Number one (Kingsbury Cottage) was missed off the King's Road census report, being counted in Kingsbury Avenue instead. So, 1 should be 3, 3 should be 5 and so on - to 47, which should be 49.]*

In 1911, King's Road was a working-class street occupied mainly by manual labourers and their families. The majority were local people whose extended families lived nearby. Two thirds were born in, or within a ten-mile radius of, St Albans. Of the 51 households, 43 had children and a quarter of these had seven or more children. Nearly half these families had suffered at least one child death.

Most of the town's major employers of the time are represented in the occupations listed on the census. Many King's Road women and some men were employed in the straw-hat trade. This was one of the biggest industries in St Albans at that time. The nearest factories to King's Road were on Lower Dagnall Street and Fishpool Street. Women in this trade worked as 'machinists', 'sowers', 'finishers' or 'plait banders' while only men worked as 'blockers'. It was the blockers who moulded the hats into shape. Some 15% of the women in this trade worked from home at this time.

Figure 45, The Dunham and Martin straw-hat factory,
at the rear of 9 - 11 Fishpool Street, 1914.
Photograph courtesy of HALS.

Maygrove's Silk Mill on Abbey Mill Lane employed a large number of King's Road women as 'silk winders' and 'silk throwsters'. One was a 'silk lacer'. Women worked as dressmakers and laundry maids. One young woman worked in a seed warehouse (either the seed warehouse west of Branch Road or the Ryder's Seed Hall on Holywell Hill), and four worked as tailoresses in the raincoat works (the only one in St Albans being Nicholson's in Sutton Road, Fleetville). One was an elementary school teacher. The majority of working women were young and unmarried. Many women with children had no occupation listed. Presumably, most of these were fully occupied at home caring for their families.

THE SILK MILL. ST. ALBANS. 35

Figure 46, Maygrove's Silk Mill c1910.
Photograph courtesy of Andy Lawrence.

Several young men and women worked in the boot and shoe manufacturing industry and in shops. The males of King's Road worked as gardeners, coachmen, bricklayers, joiners and general labourers. One described himself as a nurseryman, specifically an orchid grower. There were one or two clerical workers, one electrical engineer and two policemen. One or two worked in photographic works and motor works, the nearest being where Gonnerston now stands. One worked in the flour mill (presumably Kingsbury Mill).

THE OLD MILL, ST. ALBANS. 11

Figure 47, Kingsbury Mill c1910.
Photograph courtesy of Andy Lawrence.

A small number of men worked in agriculture and farming, the nearest farms being Kingsbury, just next to Kingsbury Mill and St Germain's in St Michael's on the site of Verulamium Park. King's Road had one cowman, one horse breaker, one carter, a stockman on a farm, a stableman, a blacksmith's helper and two journeymen butchers.

Appendix 1: Absent Voter List, St Albans District, mid-1918

(Hertfordshire Archives and Local Studies (HALS))

About UK, Absent Voter Lists, 1918-1925, 1939

The 1916 Representation of the People Act ruled that members of the armed forces should be listed in separate registers under the constituencies in which they normally lived.

The Absent Voter Lists enabled servicemen and women to vote by proxy or by postal application when away from home on active service.

They record the civilian address of the absent voter but, more importantly, they give service numbers and regimental details.

Absent voter lists can be a valuable resource if you are trying to trace details of a First World War soldier.

They often record the individual's regiment, number and rank at the time, as well as his home address.

ST. ALBANS CITY (ABBEY DISTRICT) POLLING DISTRICT V. ST. ALBANS DIVISION.

No.	Names in Full (Surname first).	Qualifying Premises.	Description of Service. Ship, Regiment, Number, Rank, Rating, etc., or recorded address.	No.
1	2	3	4	5

PARISH OF ST. ALBAN—*Continued*

(Abbey District of the South Ward, which forms part of the 58th Electoral Division).

KING'S ROAD.

4014	Hunt, Albert Alfred	Lily Cottage	895397 Dvr., West Lancashire Regt.	4014
4015	Hunt, John Edward	Lily Cottage	292696 Cpl., Northumberland Fusiliers	4015
4016	Butler, Frederick	Fern Cottage	235107 Dvr., R.F.A.	4016
4017	Jackson, Joseph John	Ivy Cottage	895772 Gnr., 384th Batty., R.F.A.	4017
4018	Smith, Alfred George	Myrtle Cottage	34171 Pte., 1st Batt. Suffolk Regt.	4018
4019	Faulder, Herbert	Salisbury Villa	266271 Pte., Herts Regt.	4019
4020	Faulder, Archie William	Salisbury Villa	202588 Cpl., 18th H.L.I.	4020
4021	Cooper, William	19	890692 Gnr., A/270th Brig., R.F.A.	4021
4022	Cooper, Arthur	19	890694 Gnr., 270th Brig., R.F.A.	4022
4023	Hart, Albert Edward	Hope Cottage	193673 Spr., R.O.D., R.E.	4023
4024	Coleman, Edward	25	170773 Gnr., 39th Batty., 19th Brig., R.F.A.	4024
4025	Coleman, William	25	146513 Pte., 58th Batt. M.G.C.	4025
4026	Pegram, George Edgcumb Hollingsworth	27	81427 Cpl., 25th R.D. Brig. (T.R.)	4026
4027	Townsend, Herbert Henry	35	890011 Dvr., 270th Brig., R.F.A.	4027
4028	Townsend, Horace Leonard	35	41512 Pte., Leicester Regt.	4028
4029	Kirby, John	37	Dvr., B.R.C.S.	4029
4030	Kirby, James William Kenneth	Fairleigh	5060 Pte., 2nd Royal Irish Rifles	4030
4031	Wilkins, William John	41	S.E./30443 Pte., A.V.C.	4031
4032	Howard, George Edward	43	202346 Pte., Royal Welsh Fus.	4032
4033	Howard, Charles Henry Spicer	43	Signaller, 3rd Norfolk Regt.	4033
4034	Saunders, Cyril	45	36465 Pte., Royal Berkshire Regt.	4034
4035	Digby, John William	Myrtle Dene	9182 Pte., 2nd H.L.I.	4035
4036	Bellingham, Ebenezer Joseph	47	197870 Pte., Labour Co.	4036
4037	Seabey, Arthur	Dunstable	T1/998 Pte., No. 11 G.H.Q., Res. M.T. Co., A.S.C.	4037
4038	Seabey, Joseph	49	361528 Pte., 801st A.E. Co., Labour Corps	4038
4039	Pollock, Edward Valentine	Rosina	470011 Pte., 581st (H.S.) Em. Company	4039
4040	Butley, Ernest	Rosina	K/31453 Stoker 1st Class, H.M.S. "Mars"	4040
4041	Saunders, Joseph Francis	53	61734 Pte., West Yorks Regt.	4041
4042	Cox, Percy William	55	28431 Pte., Royal Lancashire Regt.	4042
4043	Cox, Ernest Cyril	55	Pte., R.E.	4043
4044	Roberts, William	57	890257 L/Bdr., A/270th Brig., R.F.A.	4044
4045	Gibbard, Archibald	57	6436 Pte., Depot, Beds Regt.	4045
4046	Welch, William	59	20424 Pnr., R.E.	4046
4047	Hendry, James	61	36414 Pte., 12th T.W. Batt., Beds	4047
4048	Richardson, William	67	71080 Pte., Royal Fusiliers	4048
4049	Thrussell, Charles	6	S/34159 Cpl., 8th Div., M.T., A.S.C.	4049

15

ST. ALBANS CITY (ABBEY DISTRICT) POLLING DISTRICT V. ST. ALBANS DIVISION.

No.	Names in Full (Surname first)	Qualifying Premises.	Description of Service. Ship, Regiment, Number, Rank, Rating, etc., or recorded address.	No.
1	2	3	4	5

PARISH OF ST. ALBAN—*Continued*

(Abbey District of the South Ward, which forms part of the 58th Electoral Division).

KING'S ROAD—*Continued:*

4050	Thrussell, William John	6	203023 Pte., H.L.I.	4050
4051	Jervis, Reginald Percy	6	200183 Pte., 7th Northants	4051
4052	Ashby, William	8	32633 Pte., 6th Royal Berks Regt.	4052
4053	Roberts, Albert	10	902009 Gnr., 385th Batty., R.F.A.	4053
4054	Grey, Harold	10	WN/2-033756 Pte., 3rd Army Bus Sec., M.T., A.S.C.	4054
4055	Wood, Henry Charles	12	40733 Pte., 1st Essex Regt.	4055
4056	Jeffs, George	16	12440 Pte., 3rd Beds	4056
4057	Jeffs, Charles	16	105645 Pte., 1/1 Herts Yeo., Ireland	4057
4058	West, Alfred Edward	18	568116 Cpl., Special Signal Co., R.E.	4058
4059	West, William James	18	G/89538 Pte., 20th Batt. Middlesex Regt.	4059
4060	Heaton, William Charles	24	51009 Pte., Royal Fusiliers	4060
4061	George, Alfred Robert	28	C/K14508 1st Stoker, H.M.S. "Tyne"	4061
4062	George, Edward John	28	M2/082496 Pte., M.T., A.S.C.	4062
4063	Jennings, Frederick Robert-	28	M2/082490 Pte., 59th A.A.G., A.S.C.	4063
4064	Hawes, Albert Edward	32	J68829 O.S., H.M.S. "Hyacinth"	4064
4065	Messenger, Alfred	38	65401 Pte., 1st Herts Regt.	4065
4066	Messenger, William Thomas	38	201319 Cpl., 1/5 Beds Regt.	4066
4067	Messenger, Arthur	38	16805 Pte., M.G.C.	4067
4068	Austin, William	40	116419 Pte., M.T., A.S.C.	4068
4069	Bacon, Alfred	44	15000 Pte., Beds Regt.	4069
4070	Dimmock, Arthur Charles	56	522689 Pte., 398th H.S. E. Co. (Infantry)	4070
4071	Smith, Cecil Cannon	58	52445 Pte., 1st Suffolk Regt.	4071

KINGSBURY AVENUE.

4072	Felstead, Walter	Dagmar	29156 A.M., R.A.F.	4072
4073	Chipp, Percy Henry Tom	Wavertree	245147 Pte., 433rd Agri. Co., Labour Corps	4073
4074	Briggs, Alfred Willis	Kendrick	217914 Spr., Railway Operating Div., R.E.	4074
4075	Norman, Robert Neville	Kelani	DM2/224271 Cpl., Tractor Depot, A.S.C.	4075
4076	Davies, Andrew	Larkhill	8254 Cpl., A.P.C.	4076
4077	England, James Alfred	Woodcote	528597 L.-Cpl., 473rd H.S.E., Sherwood Foresters	4077
4078	Cairns, William Robert	2	47650 Pte., M.G.C.	4078
4079	Coker, Arthur	St. Mary's	Sgt.-Major, 20th Hussars	4079
4080	Chalkley, Richard Hubert	Salcombe	M/320465 Pte., 648th M.T. Co., Water Tank Co., A.S.C.	4080

LATTIMORE ROAD.

4081	Lawrance, Sidney William	13	1620 L.-Cpl., Royal Horse Gds. Batt., M.G.C.	4081
4082	Hiskett, Charles	27	H.M.S. "Victorious"	4082
4083	Hiskett, Frank	27	100412 Cpl., 33rd Div. Signal Co., R.E.	4083
4084	Smith, James William Rudd	43	236005 Pte., Yorkshire Hussars	4084

16

93

Appendix 2: 'The London Road Promenade'

Figure 48, The Herts Advertiser, Saturday 6th April 1907.

THE LONDON-ROAD PROMENADE.—In consequence of the receipt of many complaints regarding the conduct of numbers of youths in London-road, on Sunday evening, Head Constable Whitbread caused several officers to patrol this weekly promenade in plain clothes. As a result, eleven cases of either bad language or obstructing the highway were heard at the City Sessions on Thursday.—Head Constable Whitbread explained that the cases were brought as a warning to others in order to check this nuisance, and render London-road a fair and proper place for people to walk up and down.—Percy Myers, of 14, Culver-road, St. Albans, was first fined 5s. inclusive, on the evidence of P.c. King, for using bad language in the London-road on Sunday, whilst Arthur Peters, of 17, Blacksmith's-lane, who failed to appear, was fined 6s. inclusive.— The other nine cases consisted of summonses for obstructing the footpath.—Head Constable Whitbread stated that the police had found it useless to act under the city byelaws by which they were required to first warn the offenders, and had now resolved to take action under the Highway Act, which did not necessitate the preliminary warning.—Four lads—William Hart, of 16, King's-road, George Jeffs, of 16, King's-road, William West, of 54, Portland-street, and Arthur Crooks, of 14, St. Michael's-street—were, according to P.c. Street, standing on the footpath and larking about from eight o'clock until 8.40, when he took their names and addresses. The Bench dismissed these cases, the Mayor stating that if they imposed fines the parents only would suffer. They issued a warning, however, that similar cases would in future be more severely dealt with. —William Thompson, of 3, Hatfield-road, William Frost, of 15, Hatfield-road, and Thomas Cliff, of 18, Temperance-street, three youths of about 17 years of age, were next similarly summoned and ordered to pay the costs, as were Thomas Knapp, of 25, Grange-street, and Frederick Goldsby, of Warwick-road, two somewhat older defendants.—The Mayor remarked that the magistrates intended to put a stop to this sort of thing, and other offenders would be more severely punished.

Appendix 3: 'Our Patriotic Families'

Twelve sons, sons-in-law and grandsons of Mr and Mrs Roberts, of Lanark Villa, King's Road, St Albans, all 'serving their country'.

Figure 49, The Herts Advertiser, 22ⁿᵈ April 1916.

References and Acknowledgements
Books

Paul Chapman 'Tyne Cot Cemetery and Memorial: In Memory and Mourning' (Pen and Sword Military, 2016) (for information on WT Hunt)

Niblett and Thompson. 'Alban's Buried Towns. An Assessment of St Albans' Archaeology up to AD 1600 (Oxbow Books in association with English Heritage, 2005)

Websites

Ancestry UK www.ancestry.co.uk

British Newspaper Archive
https://www.britishnewspaperarchive.co.uk/

Commonwealth War Graves Commission www.cwgc.org

Herts at War http://www.hertsatwar.co.uk/

Hertfordshire Roll of Honour
https://www.roll-of-honour.com/Hertfordshire/
St Albans and Hertfordshire Archaeological and Architectural Society (SAHAAS) War Memorial Matrix

https://www.stalbanshistory.org/wp-content/uploads/2019/04/SAHAAS-War-Memorial-Matrix-rev-edition-290818.pdf

Pierre Vandervelden http://www.inmemories.com/index.htm

Newspapers

The Herts Advertiser, 1906, 1907 and 1915 - 1918

Western Gazette, 1909

Maps

1799 St Michael's Parish. Reproduced by permission of the Vicar and Church Wardens of St Michael's church, St Albans.

1843 St Michael's Tithe. Reproduced by permission of Hertfordshire Archives and Local Studies (HALS).

c1897 and c1923 OS. Reproduced by permission of SAHAAS.

1903 King's Road. Neil and Rachel Robertson

1910 King's Road. Chris and Jan Saunders

Photographs and Images

Ancestry UK: Archie Faulder

Ricky Barnett: St Michael's Infants School

Janet Bates: Medals and Memorial Plaque for Charles Burridge

Commonwealth War Graves Commission (CWGC): Tyne Cot Memorial; Soissons Memorial; Thiepval Memorial; St Sever Cemetery; Ypres (Menin Gate) Memorial; Ramleh War Cemetery; Canada Farm Cemetery; Arras Memorial; Pozieres Memorial

The Herts Advertiser Photographs via Mike Neighbour and the Herts at War Project: WT Hunt, JE Hunt, The Faulder brothers, The Hart brothers, The Roberts patriotic family, John Coleman, G Atkins, W Ashby and the Foster brothers

Hertfordshire Archives and Local Studies (HALS): Absent Voter List, St Albans District, mid-1918; Waiting for King George V to pass on his way to Gorhambury to review the troops, 1914; Dunham and Martin straw hat factory, Fishpool Street, 1914

Herts At War: John Coleman's grave

Andy Lawrence: Gorhambury; St Michael's Church; The Silk Mill; The Old Mill (Kingsbury Mill); St Michael's Village

London Colney Local History Society: outside The Green Dragon, London Colney c1912

Paul Peters: King's Road, 2020

SAHAAS Library: Civic War Memorial dedication 1921 - SAHAAS Arthur Allen collection; believed to be lifting hay in St Germain's Farm c1905

The Western Front Association: Dependant's pension records for Henry Hart and [Philip] William Hart, as well as George Edward Howard

St Albans Museums: Horace Slade

Ian Tonkin: Hatfield Road Elementary School, Empire Day 1909

Ros Trent: Fred Henry and Fred Henry's grave

Pierre Vandervelden: Archie Faulder's grave

Poems

John Mole. Four poems written in memory of Edward Atkins, John Coleman, Fred Henry and George Howard.

Poems to John Coleman and Edward Atkins written as a series of five poems to commemorate five men of St Michael's parish who died in the Great War whose names were added to the St Michael's Church war memorial in 2018. A service of dedication was led by Bishop Stephen Venner on 9th September 2018.

Poems to George Howard and Fred Henry written in early 2021.

Help from individuals:

Valerie Allen (niece of John Hunt), for supplying information about her family.

Janet Bates (granddaughter of Charles Burridge), for supplying photographs of her grandfather's medals and memorial plaque.

Ann Dean, Local Historian

Kate Morris, Local Historian

Paul Hart, for supplying information about his family.

Gareth Hughes and Jonty Wild, from Herts At War

Bob Little, for invaluable skill, expertise and assistance with preparing this booklet for printing.

Jon Mein, Local Historian

Chris Saunders, Archaeologist and Local Historian

Joan Stanley and Ros Trent (niece and great niece of Fred Henry), for supplying a photograph of Fred Henry, his grave and a letter home, as well as sharing their memories with us.

Simon West, St Albans District Archaeologist

Also help from: Sally Bauer, David Comley, Alison Hook, Robyn Parker, Mark Sutton, Nicholas Sutton, Clare Hopkins and Nigel Hopkins

Thank you!

Figure 50, St Albans City War Memorial, St Peter's Street, St Albans.

BV - #0036 - 030921 - C32 - 210/148/5 - PB - 9781914151132 - Matt Lamination